The Grace of God

Lenten Devotionals

Lillie Ammann

Published by:
Lillie's Lovely Little Publishing Company
lillie@lillieammann.com
www.lillieammann.com

Proofreaders:
Alice Goodwin
George Lampe

ISBN: 978-0-9665912-7-9

A Note from the Author

Each year during Advent and Lent, I follow a Bible reading plan. I journal a short meditation and write a brief prayer on each day's reading. The following year, I publish the devotionals.

This book is being published in 2020 with my personal devotions from Lent 2019. I usually find a reading plan online, but last Lent I did something different. I read through the Epistle to the Romans, dividing the book up into daily readings that took me through Romans between Ash Wednesday and the Saturday before Palm Sunday. For Holy Week, I read Matthew's account of Jesus's Passion and Crucifixion, concluding on Easter with the Resurrection. I hope you are blessed by these Scriptures, thoughts, and prayers during this holy season.

Thanks to my friends Alice Goodwin and George Lampe, fellow parishioners at All Saints Anglican Church in San Antonio, for proofreading.

Profits will be donated to Love for the Least to share the compassion of Christ with an unreached world. L4L shares the Good News of the Gospel with the least and unreached by making disciples of Jesus who make disciples (2 Tim 2:2) and by helping to meet the physical needs of the poorest of the poor. To learn more, visit lovefortheleast.org.

May His blessings abound in your time alone with Him.

Lillie Ammann
February 2020

Ash Wednesday

For I am not ashamed of the gospel, for it is the power of God for salvation to everyone who believes, to the Jew first and also to the Greek. For in it the righteousness of God is revealed from faith for faith, as it is written, "The righteous shall live by faith." ~ Romans 1:16-17

The Jews were God's chosen people, and they thought they had an exclusive claim to God's benefits. Through the Gospel, God reveals His righteousness, and it's available to all who believe, to all who have faith. As incredible as it is, God imputes the righteousness of Jesus to each of us when we believe. By our faith, we obtain righteousness—not of ourselves, but of Christ.

Lord God, You give us forgiveness of our sins, Your righteousness, and eternal life. All we have to do is to believe, to accept Your glorious gift by faith. I believe; Lord, help my unbelief. In the name of Jesus Christ, my Lord and Savior, who reigns with You and the Holy Ghost forever and ever. Amen.

Thursday after Ash Wednesday

For the wrath of God is revealed from heaven against all ungodliness and unrighteousness of men, who by their unrighteousness suppress the truth. For what can be known about God is plain to them, because God has shown it to them. For his invisible attributes, namely, his eternal power and divine nature, have been clearly perceived, ever since the creation of the world, in the things that have been made. So they are without excuse. ~ Romans 1:18-20

Those of us introduced to God through our families or friends are extremely blessed. However, God has revealed Himself even to those who have never heard the Gospel. Look at the sun, the moon, and the stars. See the beauty of flowers and hear the delightful songs of birds. Feel a gentle breeze or a soothing rain. Experience the miracle of a baby. How can anyone enjoy God's creation without seeing the power and majesty behind the creation? No one has any excuse for not recognizing that there is an almighty deity. Those who has never heard of Jesus may not know the full Gospel of salvation, but they can certainly see the hand of God at work.

Lord God, Almighty Creator, thank You that You have revealed Yourself to everyone in Your creation. All we have to do is to look around us at what You have made. Thank You that even more than simply creating the world and the people, You love each one of Your children so much that You sent Jesus to redeem us from our sins. In His name I pray. Amen.

Friday after Ash Wednesday

He will render to each one according to his works: to those who by patience in well-doing seek for glory and honor and immortality, he will give eternal life; but for those who are self-seeking and do not obey the truth, but obey unrighteousness, there will be wrath and fury. There will be tribulation and distress for every human being who does evil, the Jew first and also the Greek, but glory and honor and peace for everyone who does good, the Jew first and also the Greek. For God shows no partiality. ~ Romans 2:6-11

Wrath and fury for those who don't obey the truth, tribulation and distress for all who do evil. Many people today believe God is love — and He is! — but they think that means He is tolerant of everything. "My God wouldn't send anyone to hell," they say. But that's not what God's Word says. The Bible says sin will be punished severely. What sad news that is, until we learn the rest of the story.

Lord, You are a just God and You must punish sin. You cannot tolerate evil. Those who say "their" God wouldn't send anyone to hell don't know You, the one true God. Loving You are, but You are just as well. You show no partiality, which means that all sin must be punished. Open the eyes of all who believe their sin will be tolerated and accepted, those who put their feelings about how You should act above Your own Words. In the name of Jesus Christ. Amen.

Saturday after Ash Wednesday

For all who have sinned without the law will also perish without the law, and all who have sinned under the law will be judged by the law. For it is not the hearers of the law who are righteous before God, but the doers of the law who will be justified. For when Gentiles, who do not have the law, by nature do what the law requires, they are a law to themselves, even though they do not have the law. ~ Romans 2:12-14

We are judged by our actions, whether or not we know God's law. The Scripture calls us to be the doers of the law, not the hearers of the law. The Israelites thought they were saved because they were God's people; many people in church today believe they are saved by their church membership or attendance. But our righteousness is not determined by what group we belong to, but by what we *do*.

Holy, everlasting God, I know I am not justified on the basis of going to church. You look at what I say and do — and on that basis, I am not righteous, Lord. I do things I should not do, and I do not do things I should. Going to church doesn't make me righteous. I will never stand in my own righteousness; I need Your righteousness. In the name of Jesus. Amen.

The First Sunday in Lent

As it is written:
"None is righteous, no, not one;
  no one understands;
  no one seeks for God.
All have turned aside; together they
have become worthless;
  no one does good,
  not even one." ~ Romans 3:10-12

We all like to think of ourselves as good, but we aren't. We compare ourselves to notorious sinners, such as murderers, and we decide we're in pretty good shape morally. But we are not. Jesus told us hating our brother is the same as murder. Lust in our heart is the same as adultery. Taking a pencil from our employer is the same as stealing millions of dollars. Perhaps the hardest step in repenting is recognizing and admitting our own sin.

Lord God, You are too holy to permit iniquity, and I am filled with iniquity. My biggest sin is not recognizing and admitting how sinful I am. Open the eyes of my heart to my own sin and give me true repentance. Forgive me when I repent and empower me by the Holy Spirit to walk in Your ways. In the name of Jesus Christ. Amen.

Monday in the First Week in Lent

For all have sinned and fall short of the glory of God, and are justified by his grace as a gift, through the redemption that is in Christ Jesus, whom God put forward as a propitiation by his blood, to be received by faith. This was to show God's righteousness, because in his divine forbearance he had passed over former sins. It was to show his righteousness at the present time, so that he might be just and the justifier of the one who has faith in Jesus. ~ Romans 3:23-26

We all fall short of God's glory, of what He created us to be. At first, God required animal sacrifice for the atonement of the sins of His people. Then He sent Jesus as a propitiation—an atonement. God is holy and just, and He cannot allow sin to go unpunished. But Jesus took the punishment for us. His propitiation covered our sins, and God justifies us by counting the righteousness of Jesus as our righteousness. Therefore God is both just (because He punishes sin) and justifier (because He gives us the righteousness of Jesus). This is all a free gift through *grace*. All we need to do is to have faith in Jesus—to believe He is God's Son who died for our sins and rose from the dead to give us eternal life. We just have to say "yes" to the free gift.

Father God, I am in awe of Your love for me and all Your children. Jesus took my punishment for my sins — past, present, and future, and You attribute His righteousness to me. I do not have to do anything to be worthy; in fact, nothing I can do will make me worthy. But You, Father God, do this as a free gift. All I have to do is to reach out and take the package, to say "yes" to Your grace. Yes, yes, yes, Lord! Thank You, Lord! In the name of Jesus Christ, my Lord and Savior, who lives and reigns with You and the Holy Ghost forever and ever. Amen.

Tuesday in the First Week in Lent

For what does the Scripture say? "Abraham believed God, and it was counted to him as righteousness." Now to the one who works, his wages are not counted as a gift but as his due. And to the one who does not work but believes in him who justifies the ungodly, his faith is counted as righteousness.
~ Romans 4:3-5

So often we think to be righteous we must avoid sin and do good works. Yet, we can never avoid bad enough or do good enough to be righteous in our own power. How do we get righteousness? Simply by believing God — putting our faith in Him. Of course, we should avoid sin and do good works, but those works are the result of the righteousness that God imputes to us when we believe, not what makes us righteous. The only way we can be declared righteous is to believe in the Lord Jesus Christ.

Lord God, I'd like to be righteous in my own power, but that is impossible. Nothing I can do will be good enough to give me righteousness. Yet You graciously give me righteousness if I believe. Because of my faith, You declare me righteous. Give me a grateful heart for this magnificent gift. In the name of Jesus Christ. Amen.

Wednesday in the First Week in Lent

Is this blessing then only for the circumcised, or also for the uncircumcised? For we say that faith was counted to Abraham as righteousness. How then was it counted to him? Was it before or after he had been circumcised? It was not after, but before he was circumcised. He received the sign of circumcision as a seal of the righteousness that he had by faith while he was still uncircumcised. The purpose was to make him the father of all who believe without being circumcised, so that righteousness would be counted to them as well, and to make him the father of the circumcised who are not merely circumcised but who also walk in the footsteps of the faith that our father Abraham had before he was circumcised. ~ Romans 4:9-12

The Jews put a lot of faith in the act of circumcision, as that was the sign that they were God's people. But it wasn't the circumcision that made them righteous — it was their faith. Abraham was not circumcised until *after* God declared him righteous because of his faith. Abraham trusted God so much that he was willing to sacrifice his son that God promised would make him the father of many nations. He had waited for years for Isaac's birth, and all God's promises to Abraham rested on Isaac. Yet Abraham knew that God would keep His promises even if he killed Isaac as a sacrifice. God would intervene supernaturally to ensure that Abraham had both many descendants and the land that the Lord had told him would be his. At that demonstration of

Abraham's faith, God did intervene; He told Abraham not to harm Isaac, and He provided a ram for the sacrifice. He also counted Abraham's faith as righteousness.

Lord God, give me the faith of Abraham so that the righteousness of Jesus is imputed to me. In the name of Jesus. Amen.

Thursday in the First Week in Lent

For the law brings wrath, but where there is no law there is no transgression. That is why it depends on faith, in order that the promise may rest on grace and be guaranteed to all his offspring—not only to the adherent of the law but also to the one who shares the faith of Abraham, who is the father of us all. ~ Romans 4:15-16

God makes His promises contingent upon our faith, so His promises come through grace—not from anything we do or don't do. And everyone has the same access to God's promises. All we have to do is to put our faith in Jesus, trust Him totally and completely. Anyone who shares Abraham's faith has the same promise. As Abraham's descendant, Jesus blesses all nations, just as Abraham was promised that his seed would bless the nations.

Thank You, Lord, that Your promises rest on Your grace alone and not on my actions. All you require of me is faith, and You count it as righteousness. There is no way I could earn Your favor through my actions. What a blessing that You give us grace! In the name of Jesus Christ, my Lord and Savior, who lives and reigns with You and the Holy Ghost forever and ever. Amen.

Friday in the First Week in Lent

Therefore, since we have been justified by faith, we have peace with God through our Lord Jesus Christ. Through him we have also obtained access by faith into this grace in which we stand, and we rejoice in hope of the glory of God. Not only that, but we rejoice in our sufferings, knowing that suffering produces endurance, and endurance produces character, and character produces hope, and hope does not put us to shame, because God's love has been poured into our hearts through the Holy Spirit who has been given to us. ~ Romans 5:1-5

We don't like to suffer, and most of us exaggerate the extent of our own sufferings. In a group of several people who have all been sick, each tends to describe his or her illness as more severe than the others. College kids are triggered by minor hardships and feel they have to go to a safe space. Most of us do everything we can to avoid suffering. Yet, God's Word tells us to rejoice in sufferings because of the result to which suffering leads. If we want to have endurance, character, hope, and God's love poured into us by the Holy Spirit, we should welcome suffering.

Father God, I don't like to suffer, but I know that great benefits come from suffering. Help me to rejoice in suffering to build endurance, character, and hope of the love of God poured into my heart through the Holy Spirit. What I see as pain and tribulation to be avoided, You see a way of molding me more and more into the person You created me to be — a way to make me more like Jesus. Let me praise You and thank You rather than complain. In the name of Jesus Christ. Amen.

Saturday in the First Week in Lent

For if, because of one man's trespass, death reigned through that one man, much more will those who receive the abundance of grace and the free gift of righteousness reign in life through the one man Jesus Christ. Therefore, as one trespass led to condemnation for all men, so one act of righteousness leads to justification and life for all men. For as by the one man's disobedience the many were made sinners, so by the one man's obedience the many will be made righteous. Now the law came in to increase the trespass, but where sin increased, grace abounded all the more, so that, as sin reigned in death, grace also might reign through righteousness leading to eternal life through Jesus Christ our Lord. ~ Romans 5:17-21

All humanity became sinners through the sin of Adam and Eve. All humanity is redeemed through the grace and righteousness of Christ. The one difference is that we didn't have any choice in becoming sinners; sin is born in us when we are born. We do have the choice of being redeemed. Our salvation is not born in us when we are born. We must actively reach out and accept the gift. We must say "yes" to Jesus's sacrifice.

Gracious and loving Lord, I say "yes" to grace, "yes" to salvation, "yes" to eternal life. I was born a sinner because I am a descendant of Adam. I can choose righteousness because I accept the free gift offered through the death and resurrection of Christ Jesus. In His name I pray. Amen.

The Second Sunday in Lent

For if we have been united with him in a death like his, we shall certainly be united with him in a resurrection like his. We know that our old self was crucified with him in order that the body of sin might be brought to nothing, so that we would no longer be enslaved to sin. For one who has died has been set free from sin. Now if we have died with Christ, we believe that we will also live with him. We know that Christ, being raised from the dead, will never die again; death no longer has dominion over him. For the death he died he died to sin, once for all, but the life he lives he lives to God. So you also must consider yourselves dead to sin and alive to God in Christ Jesus. ~ Romans 6:5-11

We are united with Christ in His death, which is what takes away our sin. Freedom from sin — what an amazing gift! But more than that, death, like sin, no longer has dominion over us. Our old selves are dead, but our new selves are alive and will be forever. In this lifetime, a few years can seem like a very long time, but forever never ends. A never-ending life of sin would be terrible, but a never-ending life of freedom from sin is incredible.

Lord God, thank You that I am no longer a slave to sin. You have given me the righteousness of Jesus — forever! I can't comprehend eternity, but I know it will be joyous with You, Jesus, and the Holy Spirit. Amen.

Monday in the Second Week in Lent

For sin will have no dominion over you, since you are not under law but under grace. What then? Are we to sin because we are not under law but under grace? By no means! Do you not know that if you present yourselves to anyone as obedient slaves, you are slaves of the one whom you obey, either of sin, which leads to death, or of obedience, which leads to righteousness? But thanks be to God, that you who were once slaves of sin have become obedient from the heart to the standard of teaching to which you were committed, and, having been set free from sin, have become slaves of righteousness. ~ Romans 6:14-18

We will always sin, but we are declared righteous because we have Jesus's righteousness. But that doesn't give us a license to sin! We can't be righteous, but we can be slaves to God rather than to sin. Although we will still have original sin and we will continue to commit individual sins, we won't live a life of sin if we are under grace. And when we do sin, we will repent, never using grace as an excuse for our sin.

Righteous God, full of grace, I am Your slave. Forgive me when I fall, lift me up, and keep me in Your grace. In the name of Jesus Christ, my Lord and Savior, who lives and reigns with You and the Holy Ghost forever and ever. Amen.

Tuesday in the Second Week in Lent

But now that you have been set free from sin and have become slaves of God, the fruit you get leads to sanctification

and its end, eternal life. For the wages of sin is death, but the free gift of God is eternal life in Christ Jesus our Lord.
~ Romans 6:22-23

Our sin earns us death. There is nothing we can do of our power to prevent that. We can't not sin — it's part of our very nature as a result of the original sin of Adam and Eve. Without God's grace — His free gift, totally unearned and unmerited — we would be doomed to die forever. But, praise God, in His mercy, by His grace, He gives us eternal life. There is nothing we can do to earn it; all we have to do is to reach out, take the gift, and say "yes" to God's gracious favor.

Yes, Lord! I accept Your gracious gift, the unmerited favor You bestow upon me because of the death and resurrection of Your Son, in Whose name I pray. Amen.

Wednesday in the Second Week in Lent

For we know that the law is spiritual, but I am of the flesh, sold under sin. For I do not understand my own actions. For I do not do what I want, but I do the very thing I hate. Now if I do what I do not want, I agree with the law, that it is good. So now it is no longer I who do it, but sin that dwells within me. For I know that nothing good dwells in me, that is, in my flesh. For I have the desire to do what is right, but not the ability to carry it out. For I do not do the good I want, but the evil I do not want is what I keep on doing. Now if I do what I do not want, it is no longer I who do it, but sin that dwells within me.
~ Romans 7:14-20

Even Paul, who was dramatically converted when personally called by Jesus and who wrote a huge chunk of the New Testament, said he did evil that he didn't want to do. The sin that dwelled within him did the evil he didn't want rather than the good that he did want. How true that is of all of us! We want to do what is right, but in our own power we cannot. That is why we need a Savior.

Lord God, I want to do Your will, but the sin within me does the wrong I don't want to do. I am unable to help myself. I know I need a Savior who is stronger and more powerful than the sin that dwells in me. In the name of my Savior, Jesus Christ. Amen.

Thursday in the Second Week in Lent

For I delight in the law of God, in my inner being, but I see in my members another law waging war against the law of my mind and making me captive to the law of sin that dwells in my members. Wretched man that I am! Who will deliver me from this body of death? Thanks be to God through Jesus Christ our Lord! So then, I myself serve the law of God with my mind, but with my flesh I serve the law of sin.
~ Romans 7:22-25

I would love to be righteous on my own, but like Paul and the rest of the descendants of Adam and Eve, the law of sin rules my flesh. Thanks be to God that Jesus saves us! We are all justifiably under the sentence of death, but that sentence has been carried out by Jesus Christ. He died to pay for our sins, to deliver us from this body of death. Praise God!

Father God, You are a just God and must punish sin. Yet You are a merciful God, full of grace and love, not wanting any of us to die. So You sent Jesus, the Second Person of the Trinity, to take my punishment for me and demolish death. I know that every decision from the Trinity is a consensus from all three Persons — You, Jesus, and the Holy Ghost — because You are one God in complete union and harmony. I thank and praise You for my salvation. In the name of Jesus Christ. Amen.

Friday in the Second Week in Lent

There is therefore now no condemnation for those who are in Christ Jesus. For the law of the Spirit of life has set you free in Christ Jesus from the law of sin and death. ~ Romans 8:1-2

No condemnation! The world condemns us. The enemy condemns us. The self-righteous holier-than-thou contingent condemns us. But the only One who matters, the only One who has a legitimate right to condemn us, the only One who is truly holier than us, does not condemn. Instead, God gives us grace and forgiveness.

Gracious and forgiving God, my actions deserve Your condemnation. But I belong to Christ Jesus, and He has taken on the condemnation and punishment for my sins. I can stand before You in holiness and righteousness, not of myself, but through the Blood of Jesus. I praise You and thank You and worship You. In the name of Jesus Christ. Amen.

Saturday in the Second Week in Lent

But if Christ is in you, although the body is dead because of sin, the Spirit is life because of righteousness. If the Spirit of him who raised Jesus from the dead dwells in you, he who

raised Christ Jesus from the dead will also give life to your
mortal bodies through his Spirit who dwells in you.
~ Romans 8:10-11

Our bodies are dead because of sin, yet the Holy Spirit
gives life to our bodies. We will physically die and be
buried, but that is not the end. Praise God! If we follow
Jesus, we will live forever in resurrected bodies. We
don't know what those bodies will be like, but they will
be real and they will be glorious. But those who don't
love the Lord and take Jesus as their Savior will live
forever in agony. That part is easy to ignore, but that
doesn't affect its truth. I pray for those in my life who
don't know Jesus, so we will not be separated forever.

*Lord God, when someone I love dies, I miss them. I still miss
my parents and Jack, though they have been dead for years
(nearly twenty-four years for my dad). But I feel Your peace
knowing that one day we will all be together and will never be
separated again. Thank You for giving us eternity with our
loved ones and above all with You. In the name of Jesus Christ,
my Lord and Savior. Amen.*

The Third Sunday in Lent

For all who are led by the Spirit
of God are sons of God. For you
did not receive the spirit of
slavery to fall back into fear, but
you have received the Spirit of
adoption as sons, by whom we
cry, "Abba! Father!" The Spirit himself bears witness with our
spirit that we are children of God, and if children, then heirs—
heirs of God and fellow heirs with Christ, provided we suffer

with him in order that we may also be glorified with him. ~
Romans 8:14-17

Abba! Daddy! We are the children of a loving Father
Who loves us far more than any earthly father ever
could. We are fellow heirs with Christ "provided we
suffer with him in order that we may also be glorified
with him." We want to be God's children and to be
glorified with Christ, but we aren't usually as
enthusiastic about suffering with Him.

*Thank You, Lord, that I am Your beloved child, an heir to
Your glory. Give me strength and endurance and faith to
suffer when it's required. Let me consider it joy to suffer for
You. In the name of Jesus Christ, my Lord and Savior, who
lives and reigns with You and the Holy Ghost forever and
ever. Amen.*

Monday in the Third Week in Lent

For we know that the whole creation has been groaning
together in the pains of childbirth until now. And not only the
creation, but we ourselves, who have the firstfruits of the
Spirit, groan inwardly as we wait eagerly for adoption as sons,
the redemption of our bodies. For in this hope we were
saved. Now hope that is seen is not hope. For who hopes for
what he sees? But if we hope for what we do not see, we wait
for it with patience. ~ Romans 8:22-25

Knowing that the whole creation is groaning together is
a comfort when we're groaning. We have the hope—the
assurance—of everlasting life, but sometimes the
challenges and pains of this earthly life make it hard to
see the eternal future. But this passage tells us that,

17

because of our hope, we can wait patiently even as we groan. If we could see eternity now, we wouldn't need to hope. But even if we can't see it, we have hope because we have assurance of what awaits us. Even if we don't know exactly what it looks like, we know it will be far more amazing than we can imagine.

Lord God, thank You that I have the hope and the assurance of eternity with You. Although I may groan along the way, I know that the groaning, pain, and doubt will end in glory. In the name of Jesus Christ I pray. Amen.

Tuesday in the Third Week in Lent

Likewise the Spirit helps us in our weakness. For we do not know what to pray for as we ought, but the Spirit himself intercedes for us with groanings too deep for words. And he who searches hearts knows what is the mind of the Spirit, because the Spirit intercedes for the saints according to the will of God. And we know that for those who love God all things work together for good, for those who are called according to his purpose. For those whom he foreknew he also predestined to be conformed to the image of his Son, in order that he might be the firstborn among many brothers. And those whom he predestined he also called, and those whom he called he also justified, and those whom he justified he also glorified. ~ Romans 8:26-30

My favorite Scripture verse is in this passage. I especially like the New American Standard version: "And we know that God causes all things to work together for good to those who love God, to those who are called according to His purpose." This puts the action in the

hand of God ("God causes all things to work together
…") where the English Standard Version is less
definitive of the source ("all things work together…").
As I look back over my life, I can see God's hand
working for good in things that I thought were awful at
the time. Remembering those times brings me
consolation when I'm in the midst of difficulty and
tragedy — I know that even in trouble, God will cause all
things to work together for good.

*Thank You, Father God, that You work all things together for
my good. Even when the world looks dark and I can see no way
good can come from a situation, You are working that
situation together with other things in my life to bring a good
result. When I am looking at hard times, remind me of the
many times you've brought good out of evil. In the name of
Jesus Christ, my Lord and Savior, who lives and reigns with
You and the Holy Ghost, now and forever. Amen.*

Wednesday in the Third Week in Lent

Who shall separate us from the love of Christ? Shall
tribulation, or distress, or persecution, or famine, or
nakedness, or danger, or sword? As it is written,
"For your sake we are being killed all the day long;
  we are regarded as sheep to be slaughtered."
No, in all these things we are more than conquerors through
him who loved us. For I am sure that neither death nor life,
nor angels nor rulers, nor things present nor things to come,
nor powers, nor height nor depth, nor anything else in all
creation, will be able to separate us from the love of God in
Christ Jesus our Lord. ~ Romans 8:35-39

How encouraging to read these words! God loves us always and forever, regardless of anything that is happening to or around us, regardless of how it feels in the moment, regardless of what we do. Sometimes, we think we have done so awful that God couldn't possibly love us — but He does. Sometimes, we think we are going through such difficult experiences that God wouldn't let these things happen to us if He loves us — but He does. Sometimes, we think there are so many things between us and God that He can't possibly send His love through all that — but He does.

Father God, what a blessing to know that nothing can separate us from Your love. No matter what we do, no matter what difficult times we go through, no matter how much there seems to be blocking us. You are always near, and You always love us with a love deeper than we can imagine. Empower me by the Holy Spirit to return that love, even though my love for You will be weak and small compared to the magnitude of Your love for me. In the name of Jesus Christ. Amen.

Thursday in the Third Week in Lent

But it is not as though the word of God has failed. For not all who are descended from Israel belong to Israel, and not all are children of Abraham because they are his offspring, but "Through Isaac shall your offspring be named." This means that it is not the children of the flesh who are the children of God, but the children of the promise are counted as offspring.
~ Romans 9:6-8

God chose Israel as His people, but no one is part of His people by mere biology. God's people are those who accept Jesus Christ, descendant of Abraham by promise, as Lord and Savior. Abraham was far too old to have a child naturally, but God enabled him to father Isaac when Abraham was almost a century old — something that could happen only by divine intervention.

Almighty God, Father of all who call on the name of Jesus, thank You that You orchestrated many miracles over thousands of years so I could be Your child. Help me to live in a manner befitting the child of the King. In the name of Jesus Christ, my Lord and Savior, who lives and reigns with You and the Holy Ghost, now and forever. Amen.

Friday in the Third Week in Lent

What shall we say then? Is there injustice on God's part? By no means! For he says to Moses, "I will have mercy on whom I have mercy, and I will have compassion on whom I have compassion." So then it depends not on human will or exertion, but on God, who has mercy. For the Scripture says to Pharaoh, "For this very purpose I have raised you up, that I might show my power in you, and that my name might be proclaimed in all the earth." So then he has mercy on whomever he wills, and he hardens whomever he wills.
~ Romans 9:14-18

God's ways are far above our ways and far above our understanding. We don't understand why He does what He does, but we can trust in His mercy and compassion. Why did He harden Pharaoh's heart? He used Pharaoh's hard heart to show His power to save His people.

Thank You, Lord, that we can trust in Your mercy and compassion even when we don't understand why You do what

You do. Give me total faith to not question what I don't understand. In the name of Jesus Christ, my Lord and Savior, who lives and reigns with You and the Holy Spirit now and forever. Amen.

Saturday in the Third Week in Lent

You will say to me then, "Why does he still find fault? For who can resist his will?" But who are you, O man, to answer back to God? Will what is molded say to its molder, "Why have you made me like this?" Has the potter no right over the clay, to make out of the same lump one vessel for honorable use and another for dishonorable use? What if God, desiring to show his wrath and to make known his power, has endured with much patience vessels of wrath prepared for destruction, in order to make known the riches of his glory for vessels of mercy, which he has prepared beforehand for glory—even us whom he has called, not from the Jews only but also from the Gentiles? As indeed he says in Hosea,
  "Those who were not my people I will call 'my people,'
  and her who was not beloved I will call 'beloved.'"
"And in the very place where it was said to them, 'You are not my people,'
  there they will be called 'sons of the living God.'"
~ Romans 9:19-26

Oh, how tempting it is for us vessels of clay to question the Potter! We say we totally trust and believe Him, but when something happens that we don't understand, we wonder. When we think we see clearly what should happen, we move ahead, perhaps in the wrong direction. Praise God that we who were not His people are now called "sons of the living God."

Forgive me, Father, when I try to do things in my own power rather than Yours, when I think my way is better than Your way that I don't understand. Give me true faith and complete trust in You, so that I follow even when I can't see what lies ahead, even when I can't comprehend. In the name of Jesus Christ. Amen.

The Fourth Sunday in Lent

For Moses writes about the righteousness that is based on the law, that the person who does the commandments shall live by them. But the righteousness based on faith says, "Do not say in your heart, 'Who will ascend into heaven?'" (that is, to bring Christ down) "or 'Who will descend into the abyss?'" (that is, to bring Christ up from the dead). But what does it say? "The word is near you, in your mouth and in your heart" (that is, the word of faith that we proclaim); because, if you confess with your mouth that Jesus is Lord and believe in your heart that God raised him from the dead, you will be saved. For with the heart one believes and is justified, and with the mouth one confesses and is saved.
~ Romans 10:5-10

Fourth Sunday in
Lent

In the Old Testament, righteousness meant following God's law, which no one could do fully, then or now. However, if we believe in our hearts and speak with our mouths that Jesus is Lord, that He died for our sins, and that He was raised from the dead, we are saved. Believe and profess — that's all we have to do. Of course, when Jesus is our Lord, we want to follow God's

commandments, but, praise God, our salvation does not depend on following rules.

Gracious Lord, You justify us — impute to us the righteousness of Jesus — if we give our lives to Him. You save us and give us eternal life if we believe and profess. Jesus is my Lord; He is in my heart and on my lips. In His name I pray. Amen.

Monday in the Fourth Week in Lent

How then will they call on him in whom they have not believed? And how are they to believe in him of whom they have never heard? And how are they to hear without someone preaching? And how are they to preach unless they are sent? As it is written, "How beautiful are the feet of those who preach the good news!" But they have not all obeyed the gospel. For Isaiah says, "Lord, who has believed what he has heard from us?" So faith comes from hearing, and hearing through the word of Christ. ~ Romans 10:14-17

The Gospel is readily available to anyone in the United States and probably most of the Western world. So no one has an excuse for not believing — everyone has a chance to hear the Word of God. But there are places where the Gospel is unknown or forbidden, where Christians are persecuted. The so-called 10/40 window — the area between 10 degrees and 40 degrees north of the equator — is almost completely unreached by the Gospel. How can they believe if they've never heard? Not all of us are called to preach to unreached people, but we are called to do two things: 1) support those who are taking the Gospel to those who have never heard it, and 2) to share the Gospel in our sphere of influence.

Lord God, I pray for everyone to hear about Jesus, and I will support missionaries to carry Your Word throughout the world. That's easy to do, though, Lord — it's not always as easy to share the Gospel with people I come in contact with. Guide me to the people You want me to witness to; give me the words to say and the courage to say them. In the name of Jesus Christ. Amen.

Tuesday in the Fourth Week in Lent

God has not rejected his people whom he foreknew. ... So too at the present time there is a remnant, chosen by grace. But if it is by grace, it is no longer on the basis of works; otherwise grace would no longer be grace. ~ Romans 11:2, 5-6

The Jews were God's people, and they expected to be saved because they were Jews and followed the Law. They expected the Messiah to come to Jews alone, but Jesus, the Messiah, came to all people. God hasn't rejected the Jews — there is still a remnant of the faithful saved by grace — but they are not saved by circumcision alone. It is grace that saves us all — Jew and Gentile alike.

Thank You, Lord God, that Jesus died and rose again to save those who accept the free gift. None of us deserves salvation; it comes only through Your grace by the sacrifice of Jesus. Although I can never be worthy, guide me in Your ways and lead me in the paths of righteousness. In the name of Jesus Christ, who died for my sins and rose again for my salvation. Amen.

Wednesday in the Fourth Week in Lent

For if their rejection means the reconciliation of the world, what will their acceptance mean but life from the dead? If the dough offered as firstfruits is holy, so is the whole lump, and if the root is holy, so are the branches. But if some of the branches were broken off, and you, although a wild olive shoot, were grafted in among the others and now share in the nourishing root of the olive tree, do not be arrogant toward the branches. If you are, remember it is not you who support the root, but the root that supports you. Then you will say, "Branches were broken off so that I might be grafted in." That is true. They were broken off because of their unbelief, but you stand fast through faith. So do not become proud, but fear. For if God did not spare the natural branches, neither will he spare you. Note then the kindness and the severity of God: severity toward those who have fallen, but God's kindness to you, provided you continue in his kindness. Otherwise you too will be cut off. And even they, if they do not continue in their unbelief, will be grafted in, for God has the power to graft them in again. For if you were cut from what is by nature a wild olive tree, and grafted, contrary to nature, into a cultivated olive tree, how much more will these, the natural branches, be grafted back into their own olive tree. ~ Romans 11:15-24

We Gentiles who believe in the Messiah are grafted into Israel's tree, while unbelieving Jews have been cut off. But no one is beyond hope; anyone who believes can be grafted into the tree of God's people.

Father God, may the tree of Your people grow larger and larger as more and more Gentiles are grafted in and more and more Jews are grafted back in. In the name of Jesus Christ, my Lord and Savior, Who lives and reigns with You and the Holy Ghost, now and forever. Amen.

Thursday in the Fourth Week in Lent

Oh, the depth of the riches and wisdom and knowledge of God! How unsearchable are his judgments and how inscrutable his ways!
"For who has known the mind of the Lord,
  or who has been his counselor?"
Or who has given a gift to him
  that he might be repaid?"
For from him and through him and to him are all things. To him be glory forever. Amen. ~ Romans 11:33-36

Everything is from, through, and to God. We hear and say all of the words of God's power and might and omniscience and omnipresence and majesty and glory. Yet we can't get our human minds around them. They are too magnificent for us to even grasp a tidbit of them.

Lord God, I can't grasp You — all the attributes that I know are Yours but that are beyond my understanding or imagination. Yet I will give You all the glory I can for the little of You I can feel. I can't imagine magnitudes greater than I can fathom. But I praise and glorify You along with my Lord and Savior Jesus Christ and the Holy Spirit now and forever. Amen.

Friday in the Fourth Week in Lent

I appeal to you therefore, brothers, by the mercies of God, to present your bodies as a living sacrifice, holy and acceptable to God, which is your spiritual worship. Do not be conformed to this world, but be transformed by the renewal of your mind, that by testing you may discern what is the will of God, what is good and acceptable and perfect. ~ Romans 12:1-2

This verse is very convicting to me, because my besetting sin is gluttony. I'm conformed to the eating habits of the world instead of being transformed by the renewal of mind and making my body holy and acceptable as a living sacrifice.

Father, forgive me for allowing the sins of the flesh to prevail in my life. Guide me by the Holy Spirit and transform me by the renewing of my mind to treat my body as a holy and acceptable living sacrifice to You. In the name of Jesus Christ, my Lord and Savior, who lives and reigns with You and the Holy Spirit, now and forever. Amen.

Saturday in the Fourth Week in Lent

For by the grace given to me I say to everyone among you not to think of himself more highly than he ought to think, but to think with sober judgment, each according to the measure of faith that God has assigned. For as in one body we have many members, and the members do not all have the same function, so we, though many, are one body in Christ, and individually members one of another. Having gifts that differ according to the grace given to us, let us use them.
~ Romans 12:3-6

We all want to serve God by doing something important in His Kingdom. But He have given us different gifts, and all are important, even if some are more prominent and prestigious than others. Rather than using our gifts to glorify ourselves, God's Word tells us to use the gifts

He has given us to perform the functions we are assigned without judging ourselves better or more important than anyone else. Whether we preach to thousands, teach a handful of children, or perform mundane administrative tasks, we are no more or less important than any other servant of the Lord.

Thank You, Lord God, for the gifts You have bestowed upon each of us. Let us use those gifts to Your glory and take no pride in our position or our gift. In the name of Jesus Christ. Amen.

The Fifth Sunday in Lent (Passion Sunday)

Let love be genuine. Abhor what is evil; hold fast to what is good. Love one another with brotherly affection. Outdo one another in showing honor. Do not be slothful in zeal, be fervent in spirit, serve the Lord. Rejoice in hope, be patient in tribulation, be constant in prayer. Contribute to the needs of the saints and seek to show hospitality. ~ Romans 12:9-13

Fifth Sunday in **Lent**

Paul is giving us a list of how we should live. "Do not be slothful in zeal" jumps out at me. We cannot be passive about this; it could be easy to lose our zeal, still going through the motions without ardor, fervency, passion, intensity. In Revelation, Jesus told the church at Laodicea that because it was lukewarm, He would spew it out of His mouth! That dramatically shows how important zeal is.

Lord God, never let me become lukewarm. Fill me with zeal for You and Your Word. I don't want to go through the motions without enthusiasm; I want to serve You with passion, with fervency. In the name of Jesus Christ. Amen.

Monday in the Fifth Week in Lent

Bless those who persecute you; bless and do not curse them. Rejoice with those who rejoice, weep with those who weep. Live in harmony with one another. Do not be haughty, but associate with the lowly. Never be wise in your own sight. Repay no one evil for evil, but give thought to do what is honorable in the sight of all. If possible, so far as it depends on you, live peaceably with all. Beloved, never avenge yourselves, but leave it to the wrath of God for it is written, "Vengeance is mine, I will repay, says the Lord."
~ Romans 12:14-19

It's easy to love those who love us. It's not easy to bless those who persecute us, but that's what we're called to do. We want justice; we want fairness; we want vengeance — at least for ourselves. We want to be forgiven if we wrong someone but want to punish them if they wrong us. Only with the help of the Holy Spirit can we do what we're commanded to do: forgive, bless, and bring peace.

Heavenly Father, empower me by the Holy Spirit to bless and not curse, to repay good for evil, to leave vengeance to You. In the name of Jesus Christ, my Lord and Savior, who lives and reigns with You and the Holy Ghost forever and ever. Amen.

Tuesday in the Fifth Week in Lent

Let every person be subject to the governing authorities. For there is no authority except from God, and those that exist have been instituted by God. Therefore whoever resists the authorities resists what God has appointed, and those who resist will incur judgment. ... Pay to all what is owed to them: taxes to whom taxes are owed, revenue to whom revenue is owed, respect to whom respect is owed, honor to whom honor is owed. Owe no one anything, except to love each other, for the one who loves another has fulfilled the law.
~ Romans 13:1-2, 7-8

We tend to think that an officeholder whose views differ from our own must not be in power justly. However, anyone in any position of authority is there because it is God's will. Even evil rulers, like Pharaoh, can be used of God for His purposes. He used Nebuchadnezzar and Cyrus and many other pagan leaders, sometimes to chasten His people and sometimes to restore them. We should certainly exercise our privilege to vote and support those whose policies reflect our faith. But regardless of what we think of the authority, he or she is in that position because God wills it. If we are required by the government to take actions contrary to Biblical faith, we must in good conscience follow God rather than man. Otherwise, we are obligated to obey the laws and respect our leaders.

Lord God Almighty, sometimes it's hard to see why You give us the leaders You do, but You have a purpose for everything. I pray that You will give us the leadership we need, not the leadership we deserve. In the name of Jesus Christ. Amen.

Wednesday in the Fifth Week in Lent

Besides this you know the time, that the hour has come for you to wake from sleep. For salvation is nearer to us now than when we first believed. The night is far gone; the day is at hand. So then let us cast off the works of darkness and put on the armor of light. ~ Romans 13:11-12

No one knows when Jesus is coming again except the Father. Obviously that day is coming closer all the time, and we need to be ready when it does. We want to be found living in the light, doing the good works of faith, when our Savior appears in the clouds.

Father God, only You know the day Jesus will return, but I don't want to be caught unaware. And I don't want people I love to miss out on salvation. Help me to walk in Your light to attract those I come in contact with to You. In the name of Jesus Christ. Maranatha, Lord Jesus!

Thursday in the Fifth Week in Lent

For none of us lives to himself, and none of us dies to himself. For if we live, we live to the Lord, and if we die, we die to the Lord. So then, whether we live or whether we die, we are the Lord's. For to this end Christ died and lived again, that he might be Lord both of the dead and of the living. ~ Romans 14:7-9

We like to think we are independent — self-reliant, in charge of our own lives, doing it our way. But if we love the Lord, we can't live our own way. We are not our own. We belong to God; His way is our way. Jesus died and rose again for our salvation so we can be with Him, the Father, and the Holy Spirit in Heaven. Because we are His, He loves us and wants us with Him. And He knows what we need and He works all things to good to those who love Him.

Holy Father God, forgive me when I try to be independent and self-reliant. I know that I am nothing of myself. I can do nothing without You. Make Your desire my desire, Your Way my way. In the name of Jesus Christ. Amen.

Friday in the Fifth Week in Lent

For whatever was written in former days was written for our instruction, that through endurance and through the encouragement of the Scriptures we might have hope. May the God of endurance and encouragement grant you to live in such harmony with one another, in accord with Christ Jesus, that together you may with one voice glorify the God and Father of our Lord Jesus Christ. Therefore welcome one another as Christ has welcomed you, for the glory of God. ~ Romans 15:4-7

Some Christians think only the New Testament applies to us today and ignore the Old Testament. However when Paul wrote these words, the only Scripture (whatever was written in former days) was the Old Testament. Everything in the Old Testament points to Christ, and if we read it with that in mind, we will be instructed by it, and we will be encouraged.

Gracious and holy God, thank You for Your Word – both Old and New Testaments. Thank You that You knew from the beginning that man would fall and need a Savior. You planned for Jesus to sacrifice His life for our sins, and You gave us the Old Testament to give hope that the Messiah would come. And we know He will come again in glory. Make me ready, Lord, to meet Jesus when He comes again. In His holy Name I pray. Amen.

Saturday in the Fifth Week in Lent

Now to him who is able to strengthen you according to my gospel and the preaching of Jesus Christ, according to the revelation of the mystery that was kept secret for long ages but has now been disclosed and through the prophetic writings has been made known to all nations, according to the command of the eternal God, to bring about the obedience of faith—to the only wise God be glory forevermore through Jesus Christ! Amen. ~ Romans 16:25-27

The mystery that was kept secret for long ages was that we — the Gentiles — would be saved by the Messiah, just like the Jews. Jesus died on the cross of our sins, and He rose again on the third day to give us eternal day. Glory be to the Father and to the Son and to the Holy Spirit!

Only wise, eternal God, who offers the gift of salvation to all who will accept it, I give You glory. In the name of Jesus Christ, the Messiah whose sacrifice made the gift of salvation possible. Amen.

Palm Sunday

Now when they drew near to Jerusalem and came to Bethphage, to the Mount of Olives, then Jesus sent two disciples, saying to them, "Go into the village in front of you, and immediately you will find a donkey tied, and a colt with

her. Untie them and bring them to me. If anyone says anything to you, you shall say, 'The Lord needs them,' and he will send them at once." This took place to fulfill what was spoken by the prophet, saying,
"Say to the daughter of Zion,
'Behold, your king is coming to you,
  humble, and mounted on a donkey,
  on a colt, the foal of a beast of burden.'"

The disciples went and did as Jesus had directed them. They brought the donkey and the colt and put on them their cloaks, and he sat on them. Most of the crowd spread their cloaks on the road, and others cut branches from the trees and spread them on the road. And the crowds that went before him and that followed him were shouting, "Hosanna to the Son of David! Blessed is he who comes in the name of the Lord! Hosanna in the highest!" And when he entered Jerusalem, the whole city was stirred up, saying, "Who is this?" And the crowds said, "This is the prophet Jesus, from Nazareth of Galilee." ~ Matthew 21:1-11

Every time I read this story of the Triumphal Entry, I am amazed that the donkey and colt were tied up waiting for the disciples to come get them. They didn't have to look for a donkey or plead with the owner to release the donkey. All they had to do was to say, "The Lord needs them." Even more amazing, the Triumphal Entry was prophesied by Zechariah five centuries earlier. What an example of God's plan! The crowds spreading palms and crying "Hosanna" was not a spur-of-the-moment event; it was part of the perfect plan of the perfect God.

Holy God, omniscient and omnipresent Lord, I praise You for Your great love for us and Your perfect plan for our salvation. May everyone on earth hear Your Word and believe. In the name of Jesus Christ, who lives and reigns with You and the Holy Ghost forever and ever. Amen.

Monday in Holy Week

And Jesus entered the temple and drove out all who sold and bought in the temple, and he overturned the tables of the money-changers and the seats of those who sold pigeons. He said to them, "It is written, 'My house shall be called a house of prayer,' but you make it a den of robbers."

And the blind and the lame came to him in the temple, and he healed them. But when the chief priests and the scribes saw the wonderful things that he did, and the children crying out in the temple, "Hosanna to the Son of David!" they were indignant, and they said to him, "Do you hear what these are saying?" And Jesus said to them, "Yes; have you never read, "'Out of the mouth of infants and nursing babies
  you have prepared praise'?"
And leaving them, he went out of the city to Bethany and lodged there. ~ Matthew 21:12-17

Some people say that Jesus was meek and mild and never got angry. This passage contradicts that idea. Jesus was justifiably angry that people were using the Temple to take advantage of Jews fulfilling their religious obligations. Not only were God's people being treated unjustly, but God's House was being defiled. Holy and righteous, Jesus and the Father and the Holy Spirit are too pure to allow wickedness to prevail without showing righteous anger. God has been patient and allowed the enemy and sin to dominate the world to allow everyone to hear the Word of God. But His patience will come to an end, and those who did evil and did not repent will suffer throughout eternity as just punishment for their sins.

Holy and righteous God, Your House should be kept pure and holy. May all who call themselves Christian honor and glorify Your Name and Your dwelling place. In the name of Jesus Christ, the Messiah, who lives and reigns with You and the Holy Ghost, now and forever. Amen.

Tuesday in Holy Week

And when he entered the temple, the chief priests and the elders of the people came up to him as he was teaching, and said, "By what authority are you doing these things, and who gave you this authority?" Jesus answered them, "I also will ask you one question, and if you tell me the answer, then I also will tell you by what authority I do these things. The baptism of John, from where did it come? From heaven or from man?" And they discussed it among themselves, saying, "If we say, 'From heaven,' he will say to us, 'Why then did you not believe him?' But if we say, 'From man,' we are afraid of the crowd, for they all hold that John was a prophet." So they answered Jesus, "We do not know." And he said to them, "Neither will I tell you by what authority I do these things.
~ Matthew 21:23-27

The chief priests and elders put up a tough front, demanding that Jesus tell them by what authority He performed miracles. But Jesus turned the tables on them and asked them a question they wouldn't answer out of fear of the crowds. It had to have been obvious that Jesus got His authority from

God, and they wanted to hear Him say that so they could denounce His words as blasphemy. But He was too wise to give them that opportunity.

Almighty God, nothing man could do could obstruct Your plan for our salvation. You knew exactly how the religious leaders would respond, and You thwarted their plans to fulfill Your own. Thank You that Your plan for me and for each of Your children is perfect. In Jesus's name. Amen.

Wednesday in Holy Week

Now on the first day of Unleavened Bread the disciples came to Jesus, saying, "Where will you have us prepare for you to eat the Passover?" He said, "Go into the city to a certain man and say to him, 'The Teacher says, My time is at hand. I will keep the Passover at your house with my disciples.'" And the disciples did as Jesus had directed them, and they prepared the Passover.

When it was evening, he reclined at table with the twelve. And as they were eating, he said, "Truly, I say to you, one of you will betray me." And they were very sorrowful and began to say to him one after another, "Is it I, Lord?" He answered, "He who has dipped his hand in the dish with me will betray me. The Son of Man goes as it is written of him, but woe to that man by whom the Son of Man is betrayed! It would have been better for that man if he had not been born." Judas, who would betray him, answered, "Is it I, Rabbi?" He said to him, "You have said so." ~ Matthew 26:17-25

Jesus knew that Judas would betray him even before calling Judas to be an apostle. Yet as part of God's plan for our salvation, He chose Judas and traveled and taught and lived with him for three years. He didn't treat Judas any differently than the other apostles; indeed, Judas was the one trusted with the money box.

Holy and Eternal God, Your plan required that one man from among Jesus's most trusted followers betray Him. If I even suspected that someone to whom I was close would betray me, I would distance myself from that person and try to prevent the betrayal from happening. Yet Jesus kept Judas close and in essence invited Judas to betray – and all for my sake and for the sake of all who trust in Jesus. There is no way for me to express my love and thanksgiving for my salvation, but I will endeavor to live a life that brings You glory. In the name of Jesus Christ, my Savior. Amen.

Maundy Thursday

Now as they were eating, Jesus took bread, and after blessing it broke it and gave it to the disciples, and said, "Take, eat; this is my body." And he took a cup, and when he had given

Maundy Thursday

thanks he gave it to them, saying, "Drink of it, all of you, for this is my blood of the covenant, which is poured out for many for the forgiveness of sins. I tell you I will not drink again of this fruit of the vine until that day when I drink it new with you in my Father's kingdom."

And when they had sung a hymn, they went out to the Mount of Olives. Then Jesus said to them, "You will all fall away because of me this night. For it is written, 'I will strike the shepherd, and the sheep of the flock will be scattered.' But after I am raised up, I will go before you to Galilee." Peter answered him, "Though they all fall away because of you, I will never fall away." Jesus said to him, "Truly, I tell you, this very night, before the rooster crows, you will deny me three times." Peter said to him, "Even if I must die with you, I will not deny you!" And all the disciples said the same.

Then Jesus went with them to a place called Gethsemane, and he said to his disciples, "Sit here, while I go over there and pray." And taking with him Peter and the two sons of Zebedee, he began to be sorrowful and troubled. Then he said to them, "My soul is very sorrowful, even to death; remain here, and watch with me." And going a little farther he fell on his face and prayed, saying, "My Father, if it be possible, let this cup pass from me; nevertheless, not as I will, but as you will." And he came to the disciples and found them sleeping. And he said to Peter, "So, could you not watch with me one hour? Watch and pray that you may not enter into temptation. The spirit indeed is willing, but the flesh is weak." Again, for the second time, he went away and prayed, "My Father, if this cannot pass unless I drink it, your will be done." And again he came and found them sleeping, for their eyes were heavy. So, leaving them again, he went away and prayed for the third time, saying the same words again. Then he came to the disciples and said to them, "Sleep and take your rest later on. See, the hour is at hand, and the Son of Man is betrayed into the hands of sinners. Rise, let us be going; see, my betrayer is at hand."

While he was still speaking, Judas came, one of the twelve, and with him a great crowd with swords and clubs, from the chief priests and the elders of the people. Now the betrayer had given them a sign, saying, "The one I will kiss is the man; seize him." And he came up to Jesus at once and said,

"Greetings, Rabbi!" And he kissed him. Jesus said to him, "Friend, do what you came to do." Then they came up and laid hands on Jesus and seized him. And behold, one of those who were with Jesus stretched out his hand and drew his sword and struck the servant of the high priest and cut off his ear. Then Jesus said to him, "Put your sword back into its place. For all who take the sword will perish by the sword. Do you think that I cannot appeal to my Father, and he will at once send me more than twelve legions of angels? But how then should the Scriptures be fulfilled, that it must be so?" At that hour Jesus said to the crowds, "Have you come out as against a robber, with swords and clubs to capture me? Day after day I sat in the temple teaching, and you did not seize me. But all this has taken place that the Scriptures of the prophets might be fulfilled." Then all the disciples left him and fled. ~ Matthew 26:26-56

The disciples couldn't stay awake when Jesus was praying in Gethsemane, pleading with His Father to take away the cup of wrath Jesus was about to drink. Nevertheless, He said, let the Father's will be done, not His. Then when He was arrested, the disciples all ran away and left Him — the disciples who promised they would never deny Him. They didn't know that the arrest was part of God's grand plan and that everything would turn around on Sunday. But we know — and how often do we turn away and deny Jesus; if not by physically running way, we do it by staying silent when we should speak up.

Father, forgive me for the times I fail to stand up for You. Let me never deny You by thought, word, or deed. In the name of Jesus Christ, Who took my sins upon Him willingly and Who

now lives and reigns with You and the Holy Spirit forever.
Amen.

Good Friday

And when they had mocked him, they
stripped him of the robe and put his own
clothes on him and led him away to
crucify him.

Good Friday

Over his head they put
the charge against him, which read.

As they went out, they found a man of
Cyrene, Simon by name. They compelled
this man to carry his cross. And when

This is Jesus,
the King of the Jews.
Matthew 27:37

they came to a place called Golgotha (which means Place of a
Skull), they offered him wine to drink, mixed with gall, but
when he tasted it, he would not drink it. And when they had
crucified him, they divided his garments among them by
casting lots. Then they sat down and kept watch over him
there. And over his head they put the charge against him,
which read, "This is Jesus, the King of the Jews." Then two
robbers were crucified with him, one on the right and one on
the left. And those who passed by derided him, wagging their
heads and saying, "You who would destroy the temple and
rebuild it in three days, save yourself! If you are the Son of
God, come down from the cross." So also the chief priests,
with the scribes and elders, mocked him, saying, "He saved
others; he cannot save himself. He is the King of Israel; let him
come down now from the cross, and we will believe in him.
He trusts in God; let God deliver him now, if he desires him.
For he said, 'I am the Son of God.'" And the robbers who were
crucified with him also reviled him in the same way.

Now from the sixth hour there was darkness over all the land
until the ninth hour. And about the ninth hour Jesus cried out

with a loud voice, saying, "Eli, Eli, lema sabachthani?" that is, "My God, my God, why have you forsaken me?" And some of the bystanders, hearing it, said, "This man is calling Elijah." And one of them at once ran and took a sponge, filled it with sour wine, and put it on a reed and gave it to him to drink. But the others said, "Wait, let us see whether Elijah will come to save him." And Jesus cried out again with a loud voice and yielded up his spirit.

And behold, the curtain of the temple was torn in two, from top to bottom. And the earth shook, and the rocks were split. The tombs also were opened. And many bodies of the saints who had fallen asleep were raised, and coming out of the tombs after his resurrection they went into the holy city and appeared to many. When the centurion and those who were with him, keeping watch over Jesus, saw the earthquake and what took place, they were filled with awe and said, "Truly this was the Son of God!" ~ Matthew 27:31-54

The physical pain Jesus experienced was horrific. Crucifixion was the most vicious form of death possible, and He had been flogged almost to death before He was ever hung on the cross. I read recently that there are five kinds of wounds that can happen to the human body, and Jesus experienced every one of them. Crucifixion usually results in an excruciatingly painful death by suffocation, but I read that Jesus bled to death from all His wounds while suffocating. I can't imagine that much pain, but that wasn't the worst of it. For that short time when Jesus cried out to the Father, "Why have You forsaken me?", the Father and the Son were separated — for the only time in all eternity. Jesus became sin for us, and the Holy Father cannot look upon sin. The separation was more painful to both the Father and the Son than all the physical pain, which was pure torture. And They did it all for us! Because of that moment of indescribable and incalculable pain, we are forgiven of our sins and have eternal life with the Father, Son, and Holy Spirit.

Father God, I cannot fathom the depths of pain that both You and Jesus suffered to pay for my sins. It is because of my sins that Jesus was tortured and murdered. It was because of my sins that You and Your beloved Son were separated for the only time in all of eternity. How can I thank You both for that incredible gift? I will endeavor the life You want me to live, with the help of the Holy Spirit. In the name of Jesus Christ, my Lord and Savior. Amen.

Holy Saturday

When it was evening, there came a rich man from Arimathea, named Joseph, who also was a disciple of Jesus. He went to Pilate and asked for the body of Jesus. Then Pilate ordered it to be given to him. And Joseph took the body and wrapped it in a clean linen shroud and laid it in his own new tomb, which he had cut in the rock. And he rolled a great stone to the entrance of the tomb and went away. Mary Magdalene and the other Mary were there, sitting opposite the tomb.

The next day, that is, after the day of Preparation, the chief priests and the Pharisees gathered before Pilate and said, "Sir, we remember how that impostor said, while he was still alive, 'After three days I will rise.' Therefore order the tomb to be made secure until the third day, lest his disciples go and steal him away and tell the people, 'He has risen from the dead,' and the last fraud will be worse than the first." Pilate said to them, "You have a guard of soldiers. Go, make it as secure as you can." So they went and made the tomb secure by sealing the stone and setting a guard. ~ Matthew 27:57-66

The soldiers thought they could make the tomb secure. They secured it against men, but they couldn't secure it from God's power. All the strength and authority and power we think we have as humans is as nothing in the face of the strength and authority and power of the Lord.

Holy Omnipotent God, Your power is infinite, and nothing men can do will thwart Your plan. You are sovereign. You are in control. I praise You and glorify You for Your power and Your might. In the name of Jesus Christ, my Lord and Savior, who lives and reigns with You and the Holy Ghost, one God, world without end. Amen.

Easter Sunday

Now after the Sabbath, toward the dawn of the first day of the week, Mary Magdalene and the other Mary went to see the tomb. And behold, there was a great earthquake, for an angel of the Lord descended from heaven and came and rolled back the stone and sat on it. His appearance was like lightning, and his clothing white as snow.

He Is RISEN INDEED!

And for fear of him the guards trembled and became like dead men. But the angel said to the women, "Do not be afraid, for I know that you seek Jesus who was crucified. He is not here, for he has risen, as he said. Come, see the place where he lay. Then go quickly and tell his disciples that he has risen from the dead, and behold, he is going before you to Galilee; there you will see him. See, I have told you." So they departed quickly from the tomb with fear and great joy, and ran to tell his disciples. And behold, Jesus met them and said, "Greetings!" And they came up and took hold of his feet and worshiped him. Then Jesus said to them, "Do not be afraid; go and tell my brothers to go to Galilee, and there they will see me." ~ Matthew 28:1-10

Imagine going to a grave to anoint the body that was buried three days earlier only to find — no body! Then an angel tells you the One you seek has risen. Then, you see Him — the One you saw killed and buried — now alive! What amazement the two Marys must have felt. What awe the disciples had to feel when they heard it. No man could conquer death, but our Lord conquered death. Even though the Resurrection story is familiar to us, may we never lose our awe.

He is risen. He is risen indeed! Alleluia!

Alleluia! Lord, by Jesus's death and resurrection You have given us victory over sin and death. I cannot say or do anything but fall down and worship You! In the name of Jesus Christ, my Lord and Savior, who lives and reigns with You and the Holy Ghost, now and forever, world without end. Amen.

Other Devotionals by Lillie Ammann

Finding God in the Everyday

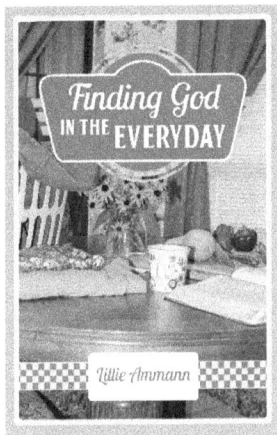

We expect to find God in church and in our private devotions. But do you wonder where He is the rest of the time—especially when things go wrong? With humor and poignancy, Lillie shares in ninety devotionals how she finds God in everyday experiences. "Welcome to the life of knowing God in the miraculous, otherworldly, plain ol' everyday." ~ Fr. Jerry Sherbourne

The Glory of God: Advent and Christmas Devotionals

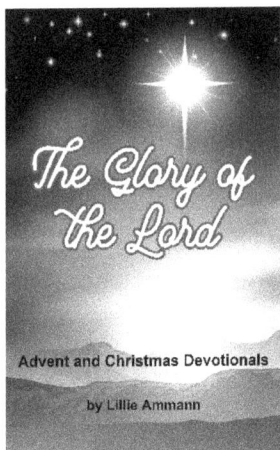

Time set aside daily for prayer, Scripture reading, and meditating on God's Word will enrich your spiritual preparation for the celebration of the birth of our Lord and Savior Jesus Christ and for His coming again in glory. May His blessings abound in your time alone with Him in these devotions for Advent, Christmas, and Epiphany. The profits from the sale of the book are donated to Love for the Least.